Isaiah 26:3-4

PERFECT
PEACE XVIII
Midnight

VANESSA RAYNER

authorHOUSE®

AuthorHouse™
1663 Liberty Drive
Bloomington, IN 47403
www.authorhouse.com
Phone: 1 (800) 839-8640

Published by AuthorHouse 04/26/2019

ISBN: 978-1-7283-0990-3 (sc)
ISBN: 978-1-7283-0989-7 (e)

Print information available on the last page.

CONTENTS

A Gift . . .

Presented to

_____

From

_____

Date

_____

*God always replace the **Midnight** of Our Existence with Light of His Presence when we remain Faithful to Him . . .*

THEME

The message of **Isaiah 26:3-4** is "Perfect Peace." This message is the distinct and unifying composition of this book with the subtitle "***Midnight***."

<u>A Song of Praise</u>
You will keep in perfect peace those
whose minds are steadfast,
Trust in the Lord forever, for the Lord, the
Lord himself is the Rock eternal.
Isaiah 26:3-4 NIV

PRAYER

Oh, Heavenly Father,
I thank you for another day. I thank you
for another day. Glory be to God!
Father, you been good to me. Hallelujah!
I pray that your people and their
families are being blessed, also.

Oh, Heavenly Father,
I ask in Jesus' name that the Holy Spirit will
help readers to remember Your word.
I pray the word of God will give them
peace, at all times, in all situations.
Thank you, Father, for blessing those
that help Your work go forth.

Oh, Heavenly Father,
Your word made it clear that You will
reward those that bless your servant.
It could be through prayer, words of
encouragement, to giving that person
a cup of water.

Mark 9:41 states,
If anyone gives you even a cup of water
because you belong to the Messiah,
I tell you the truth, that person will
surely be rewarded; NLT.

Oh, Heavenly Father,
I give you all the Glory, Honor and Praise in Jesus' name.

Amen.

AUTHOR'S NOTES

Author notes generally provide a way to add extra information to one's book that may be awkward and inappropriate to include in the text of the book itself. It offers supplemental contextual details on the aspects of the book. It can help readers understand the book content and the background details of the book better. The times and dates of researching, reading, and gathering this information are not included; mostly when I typed on it.

1810; Tuesday, 06 November 2018; This morning at 0722, I was praying in my kitchen. In the prayer I asked, Father God why am I constantly waking up throughout the night, starting at **midnight**? Suddenly, I begin to hear the lyrics "In The **Midnight** Hour" by Wilson Pickett . . . smile, that's what I did. Then the lyrics of Lee Williams & The Spiritual QC song title "In The **Midnight** Hour" came to me. I hummed it all day at work; it sounds like a book title to me. Hallelujah! I just recently started on book XVII; October 24, 2018. Father, do I do both at the same time?

0512; Friday, 18 January 2019; I have a brief thought for this
        book, still working on book Perfect Peace XVII, Arrow.
2135; Saturday, 19 January 2019
0743; Sunday, 20 January 2019

0615; Monday, 21 January 2019; MLK Day

2027; Tuesday, 22 January 2019; I just finished emailing Perfect Peace XVII to AuthorHouse. Praise God.

1644; Wednesday, 23 January 2019

1636; Friday, 25 January 2019

0703; Saturday, 26 January 2019

0541; Sunday, 27 January 2019

1702; Monday, 28 January 2019

2010; Tuesday, 29 January 2019

1631; Wednesday, 30 January 2019

1705; Friday, 01 February 2019

0722; Saturday, 02 February 2019

0741; Sunday, 03 February 2019

1628; Tuesday, 05 February 2019

1638; Wednesday, 06 February 2019

1706; Thursday, 07 February 2019

1832; Friday, 08 February 2019

0723; Saturday, 09 February 2019

0518; Sunday, 10 February 2019

1646; Monday, 11 February 2019

1639; Tuesday, 12 February 2019

1707; Thursday, 14 February 2019; Happy Valentine Day!

1623; Friday, 15 February 2019

0712; Saturday, 16 February 2019

0718; Sunday, 17 February 2019

0820; Monday, 18 February 2019; President's Day

1652; Tuesday, 19 February 2019

1718; Wednesday, 20 February 2019

1723; Friday, 22 February 2019

0623; Saturday, 23 February 2019

0630; Sunday, 24 February 2019

1647; Tuesday, 26 February 2019

2051; Wednesday, 27 February 2019

1720; Wednesday, 10 April 2019

1706; Thursday; 11 April 2019

1659; Friday, 12 April 2019

0552; Saturday, 13 April 2019

0711; Sunday, 14 April 2019

1728; Monday, 15 April 2019

1828; Tuesday, 16 April 2019

1701; Wednesday, April 17, 2019

0823; Friday, 19 April 2019; Good Friday, off work today. I will be working on **Author's Closing Remarks** and **<u>A Reader's Question</u>**; then contacting AuthorHouse. A Good Friday, Indeed. Glory Be To God, Our Heavenly Father! Hallelujah, shadomashlo . . . .

1635; Tuesday, 23 April 2019; Sending the book cover information, details, and photo to AuthorHouse.

PREFACE

Isaiah 26:3-4, "Perfect Peace XVIII"
Midnight

The book <u>Isaiah 26:3-4, "Perfect Peace XVIII"</u> **Midnight** is the 18th book in a series called Isaiah 26:3-4, "Perfect Peace." Thank You, Jesus!

It all started from how I drew near to the LORD in my workplace by keeping my mind on Him. I related numbers you see throughout the day, everywhere, on almost everything on Him, His word, biblical events, and facts to give me peace in the midst of chaos.

It's our desire for you to discover the power of the Holy Spirit by numbers, words, places, people, and things related to the word **"midnight."**

Remember, the LORD Jesus <u>PROMISED us tribulation</u> while we were in this world.

**These things, I have spoken unto you,
that in me ye might have peace.
In the world ye shall have tribulation:
But be of good cheer; I have overcome the world.**
John 16:33 KJV

However, we have been <u>PROMISED His peace</u> while we endure these trials, tribulations, troubles, and tests. Perfect Peace is given only to those whose mind and heart reclines upon the LORD. God's peace is increased in us according to the knowledge of His Holy Word.

**Grace and peace be multiplied unto you
through the knowledge of God,
and of Jesus our LORD.**
2 Peter 1:2 KJV

THANKS . . . TO THE READERS OF THE WORLD

As a disciple of the LORD Jesus Christ, I have learned true success comes when we are seeking and striving to do God's purpose for our lives. Our real happiness lies in doing God's will; not in fame and fortune.

I appreciate your support. Thanks for helping me spread "Perfect Peace" through your e-mail, Facebook, Twitter, LinkedIn, Instagram, Tumblr, Messenger or other accounts to your family, friends, neighbors, co-workers, church family, internet social friends, and associates.

Remember, you may not know until you get to heaven just how much a song you sung, kind words spoken by you or even a book you suggested reading, at the right moment, encourage a person to keep on going when a few minutes before they were tempted to give up on life and their walk with the LORD.

Your lovingkindness to this ministry is greatly appreciated.

Note of Interests: Lovingkindness is a unique kind of love. It's the English translation for the Hebrew word "chesed." This form of love is characterized by acts of kindness, motivated by love. The word "lovingkindness" is used mostly by religious traditions. The word "lovingkindness" doesn't occur in the New Testament, but words like brotherly love, goodness, kindness, and mercy correspond to "lovingkindness."

ACKNOWLEDGEMENTS

I wish to express my sincere gratitude to "Our Heavenly Father" for his guidance, patience, and lovingkindness throughout the writing of this book.

I want to express my special thanks of gratitude to E. Burton, AAO for her guidance during a **"midnight"** moment in my career, regarding my new position at a new location.

Next, I want to thank C. J. Blaine, PA-C at Baptist Minor MED at Poplar for medical care, during a **"midnight"** health crisis, regarding my left eye.

I'm so thankful for their loving kindness. The 1st time I met Ms. E. Burton and Mr. C. J. Blaine was during the writing of this book. Without their assistance in their profession, this book wouldn't be complete. You need "peace of mind" and "eyesight" to think clearly, organize thoughts, research data, scribble notes and type.

PS: Early Wednesday morning, the 17th, I was praying. I was thanking God for another day, and the list goes on. I acknowledged the ending of this book and asked Him is there anything else, I need to do or add to this book. He whispers in my ear, "acknowledge the two earthly individuals I used to help you through a "midnight" moment." Glory Be To God!

INTRODUCTION

For Those Who Want to Be Kept In "Perfect Peace"

This book titled, <u>Isaiah 26:3 -4, "Perfect Peace XVIII"</u> **Midnight** was prepared and written to open your mind to a "Perfect Peace" that comes only from God. I'm striving to elevate you into a "Unique and Profound" awareness of God's presence around you at all time.

According to some people, it's hard to keep your mind on the LORD. While most Christians will agree that if you keep your mind stayed on the LORD, He will keep you in "Perfect Peace." Therefore, so many people enjoy going to church on Sundays and attending midweek services for the peace and joy that they receive; but only for a short time.

You can experience the peace of the LORD throughout the day and every day. His unspeakable joy, his strength, his "Perfect Peace" during the storm whether it's at work, home, college, school, etc. You can also experience this peace, even when your day is going well.

This concept of this book was placed in my spirit by our Father, which art in heaven, to help me when he allowed Satan to test me at my workplace until he finished molding me into a MAP; (Minister/Ambassador/Pastor).

Throughout these pages, I will be focussing on biblical events, and facts surrounding the word **"midnight."** However, I am sure much more can be said concerning **"Midnight"** in the Bible, so these chapter subjects serve merely as an introduction and are not exhaustive by any means.

DEDICATION

This book is dedicated to the **Midnight** Prayer Warriors for the Lord.
Especially, Minister Myrtle.

I attended her **Midnight** Prayer line on September 15, 2018.

Note of Interests: The Seven Historical Hours of Prayer are listed below.

**Seven times a day do I praise thee because
of thy righteous judgments.**
Psalm 119:164 KJV

6am -	1st hour	Psalm 5
9am -	3rd hour	The Lord's Prayer
Noon -	6th hour	23rd Psalm
3pm -	9th hour	Psalm 117
6pm -	Evensong	Psalm 150
9pm -	Compline	Psalm 4
Midnight Prayers		Psalm 119:62; Psalm 134

The three prayers and hours underlined are related to the Crucifixion of Christ. They serve as a reminder of our Lord's ultimate sacrifice of Himself on our behalf.

Christ was crucified for us at the 3rd hour; 9am. Then at the 6th hour, darkness came over the land and lasted until the 9th hour; 3 pm. At the 9th hour is when our Lord gave up His spirit. Prayer is significant at any hour of the day. God has given us prayer as a means of communion with and growing closer, to Him.

PS: Information obtained from the book titled: <u>Isaiah 26:3 – 4, "Perfect Peace III," Silver and Gold,</u> chapter 4 by me in 2012; at that time, I was Vanessa Buckhalter.

CHAPTER 1

Midnight

Several statements can be said about **"midnight." Midnight** refers to the transition time from one day to the next. It's the moment when the date and day changes. **Midnight** is often called "the middle of the night," in the Bible. **Midnight** is also known by other names like; zero hours, the witching hour, the dead of night, twelve at night. **Midnight** is the opposite of noon on a clock which is a 12-hour span. In Bible days, **midnight** was considered halfway between sunset and sunrise.

The **midnight** hour is displayed in 2 different manners which are 12:00 am and 00:00 or 0000. 00:00 is known as military time, and it's pronounced as "zero-zero-zero-zero hours" or "oh-oh-oh-oh hours. Military time operates on a 24-hour concept that begins the day at **midnight** which is referred to as 0000 hours, and the last minute of the day is referred to as 23:59. Military time is also used by law enforcement, firefighters, emergency medical services and personnel, as well as hospitals.

The word **"midnight"** is of English origin and mostly used in English speaking countries. In Old English, **"midnight"** was spelled "midniht."

Note of Interests: English is spoken around the world. There are approximately 375 million people who speak English, and more than 50 English speaking countries. The top 10 English speaking countries are the United States with 95.46%, Canada, Egypt, Bangladesh, Germany, Philippines, United Kingdom, Nigeria, Pakistan, and India. English is the 3rd most common primary language in the world behind Mandarin Chinese and Spanish.

The word **"midnight"** is an 8-letter word with 6 consonants, and 2 vowels. It means 12:00 am.

Note of Interests: The abbreviations "a.m." or "p.m." when referring to noon or **midnight** is considered incorrect because the abbreviation a.m. stands for ante meridiem or before noon, and p.m. stands for post meridiem or after noon. The U.S. Government Style Manual 30th edition recommended the use of "12 p.m." for noon and "12 a.m." for **midnight**. The U.S. National Institute of Standards and Technology recommends using "00.01 am" and the date instead of **"midnight."**

Midnight is considered a compound word because "mid" is a word, as well as, "night." Compound words work together as a unit to express a specific idea. Mid indicates a middle part, point, time or position, for example, mid-day, mid-April, mid-way or Mid-Victorians. The word night is a period of darkness between sunset and sunrise, and it's used with several other words. The beginning of the night is called "nightfall."

A place where people go for nightly entertainment is called a "nightclub." A frightening dream is called a "nightmare."

In the Bible, "mid" is used with several other words making it a "compound word."

Beginning at Genesis 35:17, the word midwife is found. Other chapters and verses in the Bible where "mid" are used with other words are midwives at Exodus 1:15 and Midday at 1 Kings 18:29. Midst, Midian, Midianites, Middle, Midianitish, Middin, and Middlemost are words that begin with "mid."

The first place in the Bible where the word "night" is mention is in Genesis 1.

**And God called the light Day, and
the darkness he called Night.
And the evening and the morning were the first day.**
Genesis 1:5 KJV

The word "night" with the "s" is mentioned first in Genesis 7, regarding the Lord, Noah and the flood. The Lord told Noah to take his whole family into the ark because he was going to send rain on the earth for 40 days and 40 nights.

**Seven days from now
I will send rain on the earth for
forty days and forty nights,
and I will wipe from the face of the earth every
living creature I have made.** Genesis 7:4 NIV

The word "nights" is mentioned a total of 17 times in the KJV; 15 times in the Old Testament and twice in the New Testament. The 2 times nights is mentioned in the New

Testament is regarding Jesus fasting 40 days and nights, and Jonas living 3 days and 3 nights in the whale's belly. The word "night" isn't used as a compound word in the Bible, or begins any other word like the word "mid."

The word **"midnight"** is a common noun; it can be used as an adjective in a sentence. **Midnight** has been given as the first name for babies; girls and boys. It's considered a unisex name. According to the Social Security Administration, it has recorded 8 babies born with the first name **"Midnight"** in the United States between 1880 to 2017. **Midnight** as the last name is popular in the states of Illinois, Ohio, and Pennsylvania.

The word **"midnight"** appears in the Bible 13 times; 7 times in the Old Testament and 6 times in the New Testament. The Bible has 66 books. The Old Testament has 39 books, and the New Testament has 27. The Old Testament Books are divided into 5 sections; law, history, poetry, major prophets, and minor prophets. The word **"midnight"** is mentioned the most in the history books of the Old Testament which are Joshua, Judges, Ruth, 1 Samuel, 2 Samuel, 1 Kings, 2 Kings, 1 Chronicles, 2 Chronicles, Ezra, Nehemiah, and Esther.

Old Testament

1.	Exodus 11:4	The 10th Plague
2.	Exodus 12:29	The Passover
3.	Judges 16:3	The Doors of the Gates of Gaza
4.	Ruth 3:8	Boaz
5.	1 Kings 3:20	King Solomon Judges Wisely
6.	Job 34:20	Elihu 2nd Speech
7.	Psalm 119:62	I Will Rise

Note of Interests: The Book of Psalms has 150 chapters, and Psalm 119 is the longest psalm; it has 176 verses.

The New Testament Books are divided into the Gospels, Acts of the Apostles, Epistles, and Revelation. The word **"midnight"** is mentioned 3 times in the Gospel Books, and 3 times in the Book of Acts, also known as the Acts of the Apostles. The Book of Acts is also called the 5th Gospel because it provides detailed accounts of the birth of the early church and the spread of the Gospel, immediately after the resurrection of Jesus Christ.

New Testament

1.	Matthew 25:6	Bridegroom
2.	Mark 13:35	Be Ready!
3.	Luke 11:5	The Middle of the Night
4.	Acts 16:25	Paul and Silas
5.	Acts 20:7	Paul Spoke
6.	Acts 27:27	Paul Don't be Afraid!

CHAPTER 2
The Tenth Plague

**And Moses said, Thus said the Lord,
About midnight will I go out into the midst of Egypt:**
Exodus 11:4 KJV

The Plagues of Egypt were 10 calamities that God brought on Egypt when Pharaoh refused to set the Israelites free. The Israelites had been in slavery for 400 years in Egypt. The Plagues of Egypt is also called the "Ten Plagues," and "Biblical Plagues."

According to the Book of Exodus, Pharaoh refuses to listen to God. The plagues were punishment for the Egyptians long abuse of the Israelites, and to prove that the gods of Egypt were powerless.

The 1st plague turns the Nile River into blood. Aaron held out his rod and struck the Nile River with his rod, and the river turned to blood. The fishes in the river died, the river began to stink, and the Egyptians couldn't drink the water, Exodus 7:17 – 21.

Seven days after the Lord struck the Nile River, the Lord caused frogs to come up out of the Nile River. Moses commanded Aaron to hold his rod over the water; and then frogs came out of the rivers, canals, and ponds of Egypt. They cover the entire country grounds. Frogs were in the royal palace, king's bedroom, his bed, homes of his officials, dwelling places of the people in Egypt, Exodus 7:25 – 8:6.

The third plague, the Lord told Moses to command Aaron to strike the ground with his rod. When Aaron struck the dust, it turned into gnats, and they were on people and animals, Exodus 8:16 – 18.

Note of Interests: Although Moses was the man God called to lead the people of Israel out of bondage in Egypt, Moses gave several excuses to God why he was inadequate for this role, Exodus 4. One of the reasons was he was "slow of speech and slow of tongue." God told Moses, he would make his brother, Aaron to be his "mouthpiece" to the people and to Pharaoh. Aaron fulfilled his role. He not only spoke for Moses, but he also used his staff to put some of the plagues into effect, Exodus 7:19, Exodus 8:5 – 6, and Exodus 8:16 – 17. God later appointed Aaron to be the high priest of Israel, whose descendants were from the tribe of Levi. They continue to function as priests throughout biblical times, Exodus 28:1.

The 4th plague occurred the next day. The Lord sent a swarm of flies to attack Pharaoh, his officials and the people of his country. The houses were filled with flies, and the ground was crawling with them, Exodus 8:20 – 24.

The 5th plague was on the animals. All the animals belonging to the Egyptians died, the horses, donkeys, cattle, sheep, goats, Exodus 9:1 – 6.

Next, the Lord had Moses take ashes from a stove and throw them into the air. The ashes floated across the land of Egypt causing sores to break out on the people and the animals, Exodus 9:8 – 10. This was the 6th plague.

The Lord told Moses to raise his hand toward the sky, and God sent thunder and hailstones. It was the worst hailstorm Egypt ever had, Exodus 9:13 – 27.

The 8th plague was a massive swarm of locusts that covered the ground. The palace, the homes of the officials and all other houses in Egypt was overflowing with locusts. They ate everything that the hailstones had not destroyed, Exodus 10:3 – 6.

The 9th plague, the Lord told Moses to stretch his arm toward the sky, and everything was covered with darkness thick enough to touch. For three days, darkness covered the land, except where the Israelites dwelled. They had daylight, Exodus 10:21 – 23.

The 10th plague is the "Death of the Firstborn." This is the first place the word **"midnight"** is mentioned in the Bible. According to Exodus 11:4 – 6, Moses went to Pharaoh and told him what the Lord said he was going to do, next. At **midnight,** tonight the Lord said, he would go throughout Egypt, and every firstborn son in Egypt will die, from the firstborn son of Pharaoh to the firstborn of the slave girl, and all the firstborn of the cattle. There will be loud wailing throughout Egypt, worse than there has ever been or ever will be again.

Before the final plague occurred, the Lord commanded Moses to tell the Israelites to sprinkle the blood of a young lamb or goat above their doorposts. So, when God's angel passed over the land and saw the blood above the doorposts, no one in that house would be smitten. However, all the houses where there was no blood on the doorposts, God's angel will kill the firstborn of that family. After this plague, Pharaoh told the Israelites to leave. God's people on that very night started their march out of Egypt, Exodus 12:31 – 40.

The Israelites departure is known as "The Exodus." God introduces himself by name and makes an exclusive covenant with the Israelites based on this miraculous deliverance. The Ten Commandments make known the terms of the covenant.

God instructed Moses that the exodus of the Israelites from Egypt must be celebrated yearly, called the Passover. God commanded the Israelites to remember that significant event each year on the 14th day of the Jewish month Abib, which was later called Nisan. The Passover is a one-day holiday that commemorates the Israelites deliverance by the blood of the lamb. It calls the events surrounding the exodus from Egyptian slavery around 1513 BC.

Note of Interests: The Passover is followed by the Feast of Unleavened Bread that last for the next 7 days. The 12th chapter of Exodus gives instructions to the Israelites on how to memorialize the events surrounding their salvation from the final plague.

--------------------◆◇◆--------------------

Joshua was the successor to Moses. According to Joshua 24, he reminds the people of their deliverance. According to 1 Samuel 4 – 9, the Philistines heard of the plagues and the Israelites deliverance from Egypt; and they feared the Israelites' God. Later, the psalmist sang of these events; Psalms 78:43 – 51.

43. They did not remember his miraculous signs in Egypt, His wonders on the plain of Zoan.
44. For he turned their rivers into blood, so no one could drink from the streams.
45. He sent vast swarms of flies to consume them and hordes of frogs to ruin them.
46. He gave their crops to caterpillars; their harvest was consumed by locusts.
47. He destroyed their grapevines with hail and shattered their sycamore-figs with sleet.
48. He abandoned their cattle to the hail, their livestock to bolts of lightning.
49. He loosed on them his fierce anger – all his fury, rage, and hostility. He dispatched against them a band of destroying angels.
50. He turned his anger against them; he did not spare the Egyptians' lives but ravaged them with the plague.
51. He killed the oldest son in each Egyptian family, the flower of youth throughout the land of Egypt.

Psalm 78:43 – 51 NLT

CHAPTER 3

The Passover

And it came to pass,
that at midnight the Lord smote all the
firstborn in the land of Egypt,
from the firstborn of Pharaoh that sat on the throne
unto the firstborn of the captive that was in the dungeon;
and all the firstborn of cattle.
Exodus 12:29 KJV

The Book of Exodus is one of the five Books of the Law, along with Genesis, Leviticus, Numbers, and Deuteronomy. They are known as the "Books of the Law" because they contain the laws given to Moses by the Lord for the people of Israel. Scholars agree that these books were written by Moses, except for the last section of Deuteronomy because it describes the death of Moses.

Note of Interests: The five "Books of the Law" are also called Pentateuch. The word "Pentateuch" means "five."

The Book of Exodus is the 2nd book of the Bible, and it was written between 1440 – 1400 BC. The word "Exodus" is a Latin word derived from the Greek word "Exodos." The word means "way out or departure."

The Book of Exodus which has 40 chapters begin where Genesis left off. The history of the rapid growth of Jacob's descendant in Egypt, their deliverance out of Egypt, and their development as a nation. The Book of Exodus covers approximately 360 years from the death of Joseph to the erecting of the tabernacle in the wilderness of Sinai, Exodus 40:1.

The Book of Genesis ends with the Jews in good standing with Egypt. However, Exodus opens with a new Pharaoh over Egypt, who knew not Joseph, Exodus 1:8. This new Pharaoh made slaves of the Israelites around 1700 BC.

According to Exodus 12, while the Israelites were still in the land of Egypt, the Lord gave Moses and Aaron instructions and spoke to them concerning the institution of the Passover Feast, Exodus 12:1 – 28. The Passover signaled the new beginning of the year for the Jewish calendar, verses 1 – 20. The first month was to be called "Abib" which means "Green Ears of Grains," the 1st crop of the year. The Passover Feast also marks the beginning of Israel becoming a nation to God.

Note of Interests: Abib was the original name of the 1st month of the Jewish sacred calendar and the 7th month of the secular calendar. Abib ran from mid-March to mid-April.

After the Jews return from Babylon around 597 BC, it was called Nisan, Deuteronomy 16:1.

On the night when Israel was going to leave out of Egypt, each family had to kill a lamb. This lamb was to be eaten in a particular manner, and the blood of the animal would be sprinkled on the doorposts. The sprinkled blood marked and protected the homes of the Israelites from those of the Egyptians.

The death angel of the Lord would pass over the houses marked by the blood of the lamb and kill the 1st born of the homes not marked by the blood of the lamb which would be the Egyptians. Therefore, the name "Passover" is given to the Holy Feast Ordinance. The Passover is kept every year, as a remembrance of Israel's preservation and deliverance out of Egypt.

According to Exodus 12, Moses instructed the people on how to observe the Passover in verses 21 – 28. The night when the 1st born was to be killed, no Israelite could stir outside till the called to march out of Egypt.

The death of the 1st born of the Egyptians occurred in verses 29 – 36. The Egyptians had been in darkness for 3 days and nights before the plague of the 1st born occurred; the 10th plague. The death angel entered every dwelling unmarked with blood. In terror, the Egyptians begged the Israelites to depart quickly from them. The Israelites left Egypt with a mixed multitude, and travel approximately 32 miles southeast of Succoth, verses 37 - 42.

Note of Interests: The great exodus occurred 430 years from the promise made to Abraham by God, Galatians 3:17. God promised Abraham he would make him a great nation, and his name would be great, Genesis 12:2. The Israelites came to Egypt with 70 individuals from the household of Jacob and left as a nation of approximately 600,000 people.

The Book of Exodus chapters 13 - 24 speaks on the Israelites wandering in the wilderness and the miraculous provisions by God. God gave Israel bread from heaven, sweet water to drink, and victory over their enemies. His laws were written on tablets of stone for them by His own hand. God showed His presence to them by day in a pillar of a cloud and a pillar of fire by night.

The last section of Exodus describes the building of the Ark of the Covenant, the building plans for the Tabernacle with its various sacrifices, altars, furniture, and ceremonies, chapters 25 – 40.

Throughout the Book of Exodus, the Lord showed His people that He was not only more powerful than any Egyptian Pharaoh; He was the sovereign Lord over redemption, deliverance, and salvation.

CHAPTER 4

The Doors of the Gate of Gaza

**And Samson lay till midnight, and arose at midnight,
and took the doors of the gate of
the city, and the two posts,
and went away with them, bar and all,
and put them upon his shoulders,
and carried them up to the top of an
hill that is before Hebron.**
Judges 16:3 KJV

The city of Gaza was the Philistine's chief city at the time of Samson's life. It was a fortified city with high walls and a large gate. Scholars believe the doors of the gate entrance was at least 10 feet tall, 10 feet wide, approximately 3.3" thick and weight between 10,700 to 21,400 lbs. The gate was strong enough to withstand an attacking army.

The name Gaza means "strength and honor" in Arabic. The city of Gaza was a piece of land that was along the Mediterranean coastline that borders both Israel and Egypt. It was in the south-west corner of Canaan, a few miles from the sea. The history of the city spans for 4,000 years. The city was ruled, destroyed and repopulated by various dynasties, empires, and people.

The city of Gaza was originally a Canaanite settlement when it came under the control of the ancient Egyptians, and later it was conquered and became one of the Philistines cities. Gaza was overcome and taken control by the Israelites about 1000 BC and later became part of the Assyrian Empire around 730 BC. Alexander the Great captured the city in 332 BC.

According to biblical accounts, Gaza fell to Israelite rule under the reign of King David in the early 11th BC. When Israel divided around 930 BC, Gaza became part of the Northern Kingdom of Israel. Gaza is mentioned in the Bible as the place where Samson was imprisoned and met his death, Judges 16:21. Amos and Zephaniah both prophesied that Gaza would be deserted, Amos 1:7, Zephaniah 2:4.

Note of Interests: The city of Gaza was assigned to the tribe of Judah, and they only briefly possess it, Joshua 15:47, Judge 1:18, Judges 3:3. During the time of Samuel, Saul and David, Gaza was a Philistine city, 1 Samuel 6:17.

The word "Gaza" is mentioned 18 times in the KJV Bible, only once in the New Testament, Acts 8. In the Book of Acts, Gaza is mentioned as being on the desert route from Jerusalem to Ethiopia. Philip the Evangelist was instructed to go there, and there the gospel was explained by him to an Ethiopian eunuch of great authority. Philip also baptized him in some nearby water, Acts 8:26 – 39.

Note of Interests: This Ethiopian eunuch was the chief treasurer for Candace, the Queen of Ethiopia. He had gone to Jerusalem to worship and was on his way home. While he was sitting in his chariot, he was reading the book of the Prophet Isaiah. The Holy Spirit told Philip to catch up with his chariot. Philip asked the eunuch did he understand? The eunuch then invited Philip to come up and sit beside him, and Philip explained and converted him to Christ. Praise God!

The biblical events of Samson's life are mentioned in the Book of Judges, chapters 13 – 16. When the name "Samson" is mentioned, people automatic remember Delilah who betrayed Samson. When Samson finally told Delilah where his strength comes from, she cuts his hair off to take it away. The lords of the Philistines paid her silver.

Question: How many pieces of silver did the 5 lords of the Philistines give Delilah to find the source of Samson's strength? *smile*

Answer in the back of the book

Samson had God giving physical strength. The Philistines and their armies couldn't subdue him. Samson killed a lion as if it was a lamb, Judges 14:6. Once Samson tied torches on the tails of 300 jackals and let them loose on the grain fields of the Philistines, Judges 15:4. He killed 1,000 Philistines with the jawbone of an ass, Judges 15:15. At the end of his life, Samson pushed apart the pillars of Dagon's temple and killed the Philistines as the temple came crumbling down on them, Judges 16:23 – 31.

The episode of the doors of Gaza's gate started when Samson went into the city of Gaza, "where he saw a harlot and went in unto her," Judges 16:1. It soon spread that Samson had entered the city. The men of Gaza decided that they would wait at the city gate where they would attack and kill Samson.

The cities at that time had large gates to protect them from marauders, and enemies. The gate would be shut to prevent undesirables from coming in and convicts from escaping. The men of Gaza closed the gate to trap Samson and waited to kill him. The city gate was the only way Samson could exit the city.

The men of Gaza said, "at morning light we will kill him," Judges 16:2. They expected Samson to spend the night with the harlot and wake up the next day to leave the city. However, Samson woke up at **midnight**. He went to the gate and found the gate secured. Samson then took hold of the doors of the city gate, including the two posts, and uprooted it from the ground. Samson put the gate on his shoulders and carried it to the top of a ridge across from Hebron, Judges 16:3. Hebron was 36 miles away from the city of Gaza, and 3,200 feet higher in altitude.

CHAPTER 5

Boaz

**And it came to pass at midnight,
that the man was afraid, and turned himself:
and, behold, a woman lay at his feet.**
Ruth 3:8 KJV

Boaz was the son Rahab, and his father was Salmon. Boaz is mentioned in the genealogy of Christ, Matthew 1:5. He was born in 1251 BC. The name "Boaz" means "in the strength of." Boaz was a prosperous landowner of Bethlehem in Judea. He is mentioned first in the Book of Ruth.

**And Naomi had a kinsman of her husband's,
a mighty man of wealth, of the family of Elimelech;
and his name was Boaz.**
Ruth 2:1 KJV

Note of Interests: The name "Boaz" is also the name of one of the 2 bronze pillars which Solomon had erected on each side of the main door in the temple court, 1 Kings 7:21. The building of the temple in Jerusalem started around 833 BC. It was on the top of Mount Moriah, where Abraham was willing to offer up his beloved son, Isaac, in obedience to God's command.

The bronze pillars were designed by Hiram of Tyre, 1 Kings 7:13 – 22. The pillars were approximately 45 feet high and 18 feet in circumference, 1 Kings 7:15. The other pillar was named Jachin, and it stood on the right side of the temple door, while Boaz stood on the left. Jachin means "he will establish," and Boaz means "in him is strength." When the temple was destroyed by King Nebuchadnezzar, he took the bronze pillars in pieces to Babylon, Jeremiah 52:17.

The Book of Ruth has 4 chapters. The author is not specifically name, and the exact date of the Book of Ruth is uncertain. Many scholars believe that the Book of Ruth was written by the Prophet Samuel between 1011 and 931 BC.

The Book of Ruth focuses on Naomi, Ruth, and Boaz. Ruth was a Moabite woman who was a widow of an Israelite man named Mahlon; Naomi's son. Ruth returned to Israel with her mother-in-law, Naomi who had also lost her husband. Ruth and Naomi lived together, and Ruth would glean heads of grain in the fields during harvest season for her, and her mother-in-law to eat.

Note of Interests: According to Genesis 19:37, the Moabites were a tribe descended from Moab, the son of Lot who was born from an incestuous relationship with his oldest daughter. The Ammonites were a tribe descended from Ben Ammi, the son of Lot who was born from an incestuous relationship with his youngest daughter. On separate nights, both daughters got their father drunk and had sex with him, Genesis 19. The

Moabites and Ammonites were among the worst enemies of Israel.

<hr>

Brief Summary: The Book of Ruth begins in the pagan country of Moab but moves to Bethlehem. Moab was a mountainous tract of land in Jordan and lay alongside the eastern shore of the Dead Sea. Moab was approximately 30 miles from Bethlehem.

This biblical event takes place during a period called Judges. A famine forces Elimelech, and his wife, and 2 sons from their Israelite home to the country of Moab. Elimelech wife name was Naomi, and his son names were Mahlon and Chilion. Elimelech died and Naomi is left with her 2 sons, who soon marry 2 Moabite women, named Orpah and Ruth. Later, both of Naomi's sons died, and she is left with her daughters-in-law, Orpah, and Ruth in a strange land.

Ruth decided to return to Bethlehem, and she told her daughters-in-law to return to their mother's house and then kissed them both, Ruth 1:8 – 9. Orpah returns to her parents, but Ruth stays with Naomi, and they journey to Bethlehem. They arrived there at the beginning of the barley harvest, Ruth 1:22.

According to Ruth 2, Naomi had a close relative of her husband who lived in Bethlehem. His name was Boaz, and he was wealthy. He owned a large harvest field.

One day Boaz noticed Ruth in the harvest fields, gleaning heads of grain. He extended kindness and protection to her.

He told her to remain with his female workers and charged the men not to mistreat her. Boaz also gave Ruth food at mealtime.

Note of Interests: The Hebrew word for "glean" is "laqat." Laqat means to collect, gather or pick up. Therefore, gleaning is the gathering of grain, or another harvest produces left behind by reapers. The landowners were commanded to allow the poor to follow behind reapers to pick up left behind grains and fallen grapes. In this way, food was provided for the poor, orphans, widows, and foreigners. Leviticus 19:9 – 10 reads, "When you reap the harvest of your land, do not reap to the very edges of your field or gather the gleanings of your harvest. Do not go over your vineyard a second time or pick up the grapes that have fallen. Leave them for the poor and the foreigner. I am the Lord your God. NIV

According to Ruth 3, Ruth was instructed by her mother-in-law, to go to the threshing floor where Boaz and his men were working. When Boaz lay down that night, Ruth was instructed to uncover his feet and lay down near him. At **midnight** Boaz awoke, saw her, and asked who she was. Ruth said, "I am your servant, Ruth. Spread the corner of your garment over me, since you are a kinsman-redeemer of our family," Ruth 3:9. Boaz reacted kindly to Ruth, blessed her, and assured her, not to be afraid. He promised he would act upon her request if her dead husband's next-of-kin failed to do so.

Ruth had a next-of-kin who had first rights to buy the land that belonged to her. Boaz told Ruth, he would give him the opportunity to buy the land and marry her. Boaz laid Ruth case before the next-of-kin. The man was interested in the land but not Ruth, so he opted out of both. Boaz redeemed the family land, bought the rights, and married Ruth.

The son of Boaz and Ruth was Obed, the father of Jesse, and grandfather of David; an ancestor of Jesus, 1 Chronicles 2:11 – 12.

Question: What is the name of the other book in the KJV Bible with a female name? *smile and think* . . .

Answer in the back of the book

CHAPTER 6

King Solomon Judges Wisely

**And she arose at midnight,
and took my son from beside me,
while thine handmaid slept,
and laid it in her bosom and laid her
dead child in my bosom.**
1 Kings 3:20 KJV

King Solomon was the 3rd and last king over the United Kingdom of Israel. He became king around 967 BC and reigned for 40 years. The United Kingdom of Israel extended from the Euphrates River in the north, to Egypt in the south. The Kingdom of Israel would divide into the Northern Kingdom called Israel and the Southern Kingdom called Judah, shortly after Solomon death under the rule of his son, Rehoboam; 1 Kings 12.

Solomon was the 2nd son of King David and Bathsheba in Jerusalem. Their first son died shortly after his birth; he was conceived through their illicit affair. Bathsheba was the former wife of Uriah the Hittite who was a soldier in King David's army. David had him set-up to be killed on the battlefield to hide his adulterous affair with Bathsheba. David sent orders to

Joab, the Commander of the army in a sealed letter by Uriah to put Uriah where the fighting was the worst, so he could be smitten, and die, 2 Samuel 11:15.

The name "Solomon" means "peaceful." He wrote the Book of Song of Solomon, Ecclesiastes and much of the Book of Proverbs. During Solomon reigned, Israel lived in safety, prosperity, and peace. King Solomon was known for his wisdom, wealth, songs, and many writings. He completed many building projects, 1 Kings 7, 1 Kings 9. He built a fleet of ships, 1 Kings 9, 1 Kings 10. King Hiram's ships brought King Solomon tons of gold, juniper wood, and jewels from the country Ophir, 1 Kings 10.

King Solomon was also known for his many wives which were over 1,000; 700 princesses, and 300 concubines. These foreign women led Solomon to public idolatry in his old age; that greatly angered God, 1 Kings 11:1 – 13.

King Solomon is known as the king who built the 1st Jewish Temple around 957 BC, under the instructions and provisions of his father, David, 1 Kings 6, 1 Chronicles 22.

The Book of 1 Kings has 22 books. Chapters 1 – 12 of 1st Kings surrounds King Solomon. According to 1 Kings 3, Solomon asks for wisdom, and at Gibeon, the Lord appeared to Solomon during the night in a dream.

Note of Interests: Gibeon was approximately 6 miles northwest of Jerusalem. A delegation from Gibeon tricked Joshua into making a peace treaty with them, Joshua 9. Scholar believes the inhabitants of Gibeon descended from the Hivites, the descendants from Ham's son named Canaan, Joshua 11:9.

After the division of the land among the tribes, Gibeon became a part of Benjamin, Joshua18:25. When King Saul broke the peace treaty given to the Gibeonites by Joshua, they demanded revenge on the house of Saul, 2 Samuel 21. King David allowed 7 of Saul's sons to be hanged by the Gibeonites, and afterward, the Gibeonites are no longer mentioned in the Bible.

One night the Lord appeared to Solomon in a dream. In the dream, the Lord told Solomon to ask for whatever he wants, and he would grant it. Solomon asked the Lord to provide him with a discerning heart to govern the people, and wisdom to distinguish between right and wrong among them, 1 Kings 3:9. The Lord was pleased with Solomon request and gave Solomon wisdom along with wealth and honor. When Solomon returned to Jerusalem, he stood before the "Ark of the Lord's Covenant" and sacrificed burnt offerings, fellowship offerings, and gave a feast for all his court.

Note of Interests: In Exodus 25, the Lord commanded Moses to build the Ark of the Covenant. The Ark of the Covenant is also known as the Ark of the Testimony. It was a gold-covered wooden chest with a lid, and measured 2 ½ cubits in length, 1 ½ in breadth, and 1 ½ in height; 52 x 31 x 31 inches. Inside the Ark of the Covenant were the 2 stone tablets of the Ten Commandments, Aaron's rod, and a pot of manna.

Beginning at 1 King 3:16 - 28, King Solomon judges wisely, when 2 women that were harlots came to him. One woman told Solomon that she and the other woman lived in the same house. They were both pregnant, and she had her baby while she was there with her; then three days later, she gave birth to her baby boy.

One night while this woman was asleep with her baby, she accidentally laid on him, and the baby died. Around **midnight** this woman rose and took her son from her bosom and carried him to her bed, then she laid her dead son in her bosom.

In the morning when she rose to feed her child, behold, he was dead. When she looked at him closely, she saw that he was not her baby. But the other woman said, "No! The dead baby is not her baby, but the baby that is alive is her!" Then the first woman said, "No, she is wrong!" The dead baby is hers! The one that is still alive is mine." So, the 2 women begin to argue, back and forward.

King Solomon said, "Each of you says that the living baby is your own and the dead baby belongs to the other woman." King Solomon told his servant to get a sword, and cut the living baby in two pieces, and give one half of the baby to each woman."

The mother of the living child loved her son and said to King Solomon, "Please sir, don't kill the baby! Give him to her." The other woman said, "Let it be neither mine nor thine, but divide it."

Immediately, King Solomon said, "Stop, don't kill the baby. Give the baby to the woman who said, "don't kill the baby, give him to the other woman; for she is the real mother."

And all Israel heard of the judgment
which the king had judged;
and they feared the king:
for they saw that the wisdom of God
was in him, to do judgment.
1 Kings 3:28 KJV

CHAPTER 7

Elihu 2ⁿᵈ Speech

**In a moment shall they die,
and the people shall be troubled at midnight,
and pass away: and the mighty shall
be taken away without hand.**
Job 34:20 KJV

The name "Elihu" means "He is my God." Elihu, the son of Barakel, is mentioned in the Book of Job. He is described as one of Job's friend. The name "Barakel" is spelled "Barachel" in the KJV. Scholars believe Elihu, the son of Barakel is a descended from Buz who appear to be from the line of Abraham; the nephew of Abraham, Genesis 22:20 – 21.

Note of Interests: The name Elihu belongs to 4 other individuals in the Bible;

1. 1 Samuel 1:1, The Grandfather of Elkanah
2. 1 Chronicles 12:20, A Warrior who join David's Army
3. 1 Chronicles 26:7, The Son of Shemaiah
4. 1 Chronicles 27:18, The Brother of David

Elihu, the son of Barachel the Buzite was one of Job's friends. He was an Edomite who had traveled from Edom to join the other three friends of Job. They came to comfort Job in his time of suffering.

Elihu is a younger man who enters the discourse with Job concerning his suffering after the other 3 men speak. Elihu discourse is in chapters 32 – 37 of Job.

Question: What was the names of the 1st three friends of Job? *Smile*

answer in the back of the book

1.   E_____
2.   Bi_____
3.   Zop_____

Note of Interests: Job's four friends claim that God always brings punishment to the wicked and blessings to the righteous. Job's friends try to get him to admit he has sinned. God rebukes three of Job's friends, but not Elihu. God restores Job's life and livelihood.

The Book of Job has 42 chapters. It's labeled as one of the "Wisdom Books" of the Old Testament. The other "Wisdom Books" are Proverbs, Ecclesiastes, and the Song of Solomon. The name of the book of Job comes from the main character in the book, Job. However, Job is not the author of the book, the author and the exact date of the book is uncertain.

The Book of Job is a book that demonstrates and touches on faith, friends, patience, persistence, suffering, and being restored. The Book of Job shows God's love, displays God's sovereignty, and give insight into Satan's limited capacities, regarding God.

The Book of Job begins with 2 introductory chapters. Chapters 3 – 37 form the main body of the book which is a dialogue between Job and his friends. Chapters 38 – 41 contains God's response to their arguments. The book ends with a final narrative that tells what happens to Job after the discussions had ended, chapter 42.

Elihu speech to Job begins in Job 32 and last to chapter 37. He gives the last and longest speech to Job. According to Job 32, Elihu has been listening to Job's 3 friends discourse to Job without engaging in the dialogue. Instead of comforting Job, these friends go into a long discussion to tell Job the reason for his suffering. Elihu was younger than the other three men and had held his peace, Job 32:4 – 7. He tells them he is ready to speak and focuses his response on rebuking Job's three friends, first.

In Job 33, Elihu addresses Job. He tells Job to listen to his speeches. Elihu proceeds to expound upon the meaning of suffering. Elihu is the only friend of Job to address him by name; Job 32:12, Job 33:1, Job 33:31, Job 37:14.

In Job 34 is where Elihu's second speech begins. Elihu defends God's ability to judge fair and just. Elihu explains that God is righteous. This speech contains two sections; one section is addressed to the friends of Job, verses 2 – 15, and the other section is addressed to Job, verses 16 – 37.

The 20th verse of Job 34 is part of Elihu's speech reproving Job. Beginning at verse 19, Elihu tells Job that God doesn't care how great a person may be, nor pay more attention to the rich than the poor because He made them all. Then the 20th verse explains what happens to all people, the powerful rulers, the great, the mighty, the wealthy and the poor. It reads:

In a moment die.
In the middle of the night they pass away;
The mighty are removed without human hand.
Job 34:20 NLT

Elihu's 3rd speech is in Job 35, and there Elihu turns again to Job in condemnation. This speech can be divided into 2 sections, verses 1 – 8 deal with the so-called benefits of serving God, and verses 9 – 16 deal with the fact that God doesn't answer people who call upon Him.

Elihu's 4th and final speech is contained in Job 36 – 37. Elihu speaks about God's greatness. He declares the many attributes of God. Elihu states, "Look, God is greater than we can understand. His years cannot be counted," Job 36:26.

In summary, Elihu condemns Job's friends and Job's claim of being without sin. He declares God is just, condemns Job's attitude toward God, and exalts God's greatness. Elihu's four-part speech is followed by God breaking His silence to speak to them all. In Job 42:7, the Lord rebuked Eliphaz, Bildad, and Zophar. Elihu is not rebuked by God, nor is he mentioned again after he finishes his speech.

CHAPTER 8

I Will Rise

At midnight I will rise to give thanks
unto thee because of
thy righteous judgments.
Psalm 119:62 KJV

The Book of Psalms is a collection of 150 psalms. A psalm is a sacred spiritual poem meant to be sung, set to a piece of music written under the guidance and inspiration of the Lord.

The Book of Psalms covers approximately 1,000 years of history. It begins with the life of Moses (1526 – 1406 BC) in the wilderness to Ezra, 4th BC. The authors of Psalms are David, Asaph, the sons of Korah, Solomon, Heman the Ezrahite, Ethan the Ezrahite, and Moses. There are about 51 Psalms in which the author is unknown.

Scholars know for sure David wrote 73 psalms, at least. They are Psalms 3 – 9, Psalms 11 – 41, Psalms 51 – 65, Psalms 68 – 70, Psalm 86, Psalm 101, Psalm 103, Psalms 108 – 110, Psalm 122, Psalm 124, Psalm 131, Psalm 133, and Psalms 138 – 145.

The Psalms of Asaph are 12 psalms; Psalm 50, and 73 – 83. Asaph was one of King David's worship leaders in the tabernacle. He was a seer, and according to 2 Chronicles 29:30, Asaph and David were excellent singers and poets.

The sons of Korah's wrote 11 psalms. They expressed a longing for God and a spirit of thankfulness to the Almighty. These poetic songs are Psalms 42 – 50, 62, and 72 – 85.

Heman the Ezrahite is the author of Psalm 88. Heman was the grandson of Samuel. Ethan the Ezrahite is the author of Psalm 89. According to 1 Kings 4:31, Ethan the Ezrahite was a wise man, but not as wise as King Solomon.

Moses wrote the 90th Psalm called "A Prayer of Moses, the man of God." This Psalm is the oldest psalm in the Book of Psalms written around 1440 BC. Moses focused on God's greatness, our weakness, and the need for the Lord daily provisions.

The Book of Psalms is divided into 5 sections. The reason(s) for the Book of Psalms division is uncertain. Jewish Midrash traditions suggest that the division is based on the 5 books of the Torah; Genesis to Deuteronomy.

Each section in the Book of Psalms ends with a doxology or a song of praise. In other words, the final verse of each section ends with "Amen," or "Praise the Lord!"

The Book of Psalms is divided as follow, along with its final verse(s):

Section 1: Psalms 1 – 41
> Blessed be the Lord God of Israel for
> everlasting, and to everlasting.
> Amen, and Amen.
> Psalm 41:13 KJV

Section 2: Psalms 42 – 72
> And blessed be his glorious name for ever:
> and let the whole earth be filled with glory; Amen, and Amen.
> The prayers of David the son of Jesse are ended.
> Psalm 72:19 – 20 KJV

Section 3: Psalms 73 – 89
> Blessed be the Lord for evermore. Amen, and Amen.
> Psalm 89:52 KJV

Section 4: Psalms 90 – 106
> Blessed be the Lord God of Israel for
> everlasting to everlasting:
> and let all the people say, Amen. Praise ye the Lord.
> Psalm 106:48 KJV

Section 5: Psalms 107 – 150
> Let everything that hath breath praise
> the Lord. Praise ye the Lord.
> Psalm 150:6 KJV

The Book of Psalms is a book of prayer, praise, and perfect peace. Psalms elaborate on every imaginable thing in life. The Book of Psalms covers various ranges of human emotions, experiences, occurrences, and situations. It speaks on God's majesty, sovereignty, and creation. Psalms exalt God, encourages mankind to trust in the Lord and to remember there is strength in him. The Book of Psalms examine the past, reflect on God's character, recall God's promises, and mankind can expect God to answer requests and act on our behalf.

Note of Interests: There are approximately 219 Old Testament quotations used in the New Testament, and 116 of them are from the Book of Psalms.

Psalm 119 is the longest psalm with 176 verses. The greatness of God's word and the affliction of man are the major themes of Psalm119. The title given to this Psalm by scholars is "In Praise of the Law of the Lord." It is considered a written meditation of the "Law of the Lord" with many different facets.

The author of Psalm 119 is not mentioned, but most scholars believe that it was written by David, Ezra or Daniel. Throughout Psalm 119, he reflects on suffering and difficulties in his life. He mentioned plots, slanders, and taunts, and he speaks about persecutions, hardship, and afflictions.

The 119th chapter of Psalm is an alphabetic acrostic poem. There are 176 verses in Psalm 119 which is divided into 22 stanzas. One stanza is for each letter of the Hebrew alphabet, and each stanza has 8 verses. The Hebrew alphabet consists of 22 letters; 22 stanzas x 8 verses = 176 verses.

Psalm 119:62 is where the word **"midnight"** is mention. It falls under Heth, the 8th letter in the Hebrew alphabet which are verses 57 – 64. Those 8 verses can be outlined as follow.

Thou Art My Portion, verses 57 – 60
The Wicked have Robbed Me, verses 61 – 63

**At midnight
I will rise to give thanks unto thee because
of thy righteous judgments.**
Psalms 119:62 KJV

The last verse of this stanza reads, **"The earth, Oh Lord, is full of thy mercy: teach me thy statutes,"** Psalms 119:64 KJV.

Note of Interests: Psalms 119 contains one of the most memorized verses from the Bible.

**Thy word is a lamp unto my feet,
and a light unto my path.**
Psalm 119:105 KJV

CHAPTER 9

Bridegroom

**And at midnight there was a cry made,
Behold, the bridegroom cometh; go yet out to meet him.**
Matthew 25:6 KJV

A bridegroom is a man who will soon be married or just recently married. Nowadays, he is just called a "groom." The word "bridegroom" dates back to the year 1604, and it's derived from the Old English word "brydguma" which is a combination of "bryd" which means "bride," and "guma" which means "man."

There are many types and styles of weddings based on traditions, religion, social class, ethnic groups, countries, customs. The best man and groomsmen customarily attend a bridegroom at many weddings. The best man is the assistant to the groom at the wedding. He keeps the wedding rings safe until the ceremony, he stands next to the groom, acts as a legal witness to the marriage, and gives a speech at the reception.

The bridegroom's groomsmen help guests find their places before the ceremony. They greet and talks with guests. They had been known to dance with unaccompanied guests or bridesmaids. They also stand near the groom during the wedding ceremony.

Most wedding ceremony there is usually one best man, and up to 6 groomsmen depending on the wedding size.

The word "bridegroom" is used in the Bible as a metaphor for Christ. The church is likened to a bride with Christ as her "bridegroom," Ephesians 5:25 – 27. The word "bridegroom" is mentioned in the Old and New Testament in the KJV Bible.

Note of Interests: A metaphor is a "figure of speech" in which a word or phrase refers to being the same as a thing, object, or action. There is a total of 105 "figure of speech." However, the top 5 are simile, metaphor, hyperbole, personification, and synecdoche.

The King James Bible has 66 books. There are 39 books in the Old Testament, and 27 books in the New Testament. The word "bridegroom" is mentioned 22 times in the Bible. The word is mentioned 8 times in 8 verses in the Old Testament, and 16 times in 12 verses in the New Testament. The word "bridegroom" is mentioned the most in chapter 25 of Matthew surrounding the word **"midnight."**

Note of Interests: John the Baptist revealed Jesus as the Lamb of God in John 1:29. John revealed Jesus as the bridegroom in John 3:29. John states, "He that hath the bride is the bridegroom: but the friend of the bridegroom, which standeth and heareth him, rejoiceth greatly because of the bridegroom's voice: this my joy, therefore, is fulfilled." Scholars viewed John the Baptist as the best man for Jesus.

The 25th chapter of Matthew consists of 3 parables of Jesus which are listed below. They analyze, examine, and explain in detail the procedure and preparation required to enter heaven. The word **"midnight"** is mentioned in the first parable.

1. The Parable of Ten Virgin Bridesmaids, verses 1 - 13
2. The Parable of the 3 Servants, Who were given Talents, verses 14 - 30
3. The Parable of the Final Judgment by the Son of Man, verses 31 – 46

According to Matthew 25, Jesus spoke another parable to the disciples. The "Kingdom of Heaven" is like what happened to10 young virgins who took their oil lamps and went to a wedding to meet the groom. Jesus said, "five were foolish, and five were wise." The foolish took their lamps but didn't take any extra oil, but the wise took extra oil for their oil lamps.

Note of Interests: Even though there are approximately 15 biblical oils in the Bible, scholars believe olive oil was the oil used in the lamps of the bridesmaids. Olive oil was widely used during the Bible era. It was used as an ointment for anointing the living and the dead. It was given as a sacred offering. It was used for lighting lamps in the Tabernacle, Temple, and ordinary people's homes. Olive oil was used for cooking, health remedies, personal grooming, and an ingredient in soap. The words "olive oil" are used figuratively for the Holy Spirit.

PS: The other oils are listed in the back of the book for your reading pleasure. smile

While the bridegroom tarry, the 10 bridesmaids grew tired and fell asleep. According to Matthew 25:6, at **midnight** they were awakened by a loud shout, "Behold, here is the bridegroom! Come out to meet him!" They arose and adjusted their lamps.

The 5 foolish bridesmaids realized their lamps were low on oil. They asked the 5 wise bridesmaids to give them some of their oil because their lamps were going out. The 5 wise bridesmaids said, no because they feared they then wouldn't have enough for themselves. The 5 foolish were told to go and buy some for themselves. When they had left to buy oil, the bridegroom arrived.

The 5 bridesmaids that were ready went in with him to the wedding, and then the doors were shut. Later, the other bridesmaids returned. They stood outside the doors calling, "Lord! Lord! Open the door for us!" He replied, "Truly I tell you, I know you not."

The last verse of this parable reads:

Watch therefore,
for ye know neither the day nor the hour
wherein the Son of man cometh.
Matthew 25:13 KJV

Therefore, keep watch because you do
not know the day or the hour.
Matthew 25:13 NIV

So you, too, must keep watch!
For you do not know the day or hour of my return.
Matthew 25:13 NLT

CHAPTER 10

Be Ready!

**Watch ye therefore: for ye know not when
the master of the house cometh,
at even, or at midnight, or at the
cockcrowing, or in the morning.**
Mark 13:35 KJV

The Gospel According to Mark is one of the 4 Canonical Gospels in the New Testament. The 4 Canonical Gospels are Matthew, Mark, Luke, and John which were written between 70 AD and 100 AD. These gospel books are traditionally considered a significant part of the religion official text.

The Gospel According to Mark is also one of the 3 Synoptic Gospels. The 3 Synoptic Gospels are Matthew, Mark, and Luke. The recorded biblical events in these gospels are some of the same biblical stories, in a similar sequence and sometimes in identical wording. The 4 Gospels tell the ministry of Jesus from his baptism by John the Baptist, to his death, burial, and the discovery of the empty tomb.

The early church believes that the Gospel of Mark was written by John Mark who is also known as Mark. Mark was a close traveling companion of Peter, from whom he received the tradition of the biblical events said and performed by Jesus. Scholars widely accepted that Mark's Gospel was also a source for the Gospels of Matthew and Luke.

Note of Interests: Other traveling companions of Paul from time to time were Barnabas, Silas, Luke, and Timothy. In Paul's letters, he also mentioned Gaius, Aristarchus, Epaphroditus; Acts 19:29 and Philippians 2:25.

The first mention of Mark is in Acts 12. He is mentioned with his mother, Mary. She had a house in Jerusalem that served as a meeting place for believers, Acts 12:12. When Paul and Barnabas returned to Antioch from Jerusalem after the famine visit, Mark accompanied them, Acts 12:25.

In Acts 13, Mark appears as a helper to Paul and Barnabas on their first missionary journey. However, Mark deserted them at Perga in Pamphylia to return to Jerusalem, Acts 13:13. When Barnabas proposed taking Mark on the 2nd missionary journey, Paul refused. Barnabas took Mark, who is his cousin and departed for Cyprus, Colossian 4:10. There is no further mention of either Mark or Barnabas in the Book of Acts.

Mark reappears in Paul's letter to the Colossians written from Rome. Paul sent a greeting from Mark and said, "You have received instructions about him; if he comes to you, welcome him," Colossians 4:10. Toward the end of Paul's life, Mark had become an enormous help to Paul in his ministry, 2 Timothy 4:11.

Only Luke is with me.
Get Mark and bring him with you, because
he is helpful to me in my ministry.
2 Timothy 4:11 NIV

The Gospel of Mark has 16 chapters. It was written to prove that Jesus Christ is the Messiah, the Son of God who was sent to suffer, serve, rescue and restore mankind. The Gospel of Mark has an action-packed sequence of events that focus on Jesus' miracles and His divine Sonship.

The 16 chapters of the Gospel of Mark can be divided into two segments. In Mark 1 – 7, Jesus is traveling north and preaching until chapter 8. Then in Chapters 8 – 16, Jesus is traveling south, back to Jerusalem.

The Gospel of Mark, 1st chapter begins with John the Baptist preparing the way for the ministry of Jesus by preaching in the wilderness. Jesus comes to John to be baptized in the Jordan River. Jesus is tested by Satan in the wilderness. After the wilderness experience, Jesus begins his ministry by preaching the gospel of the Kingdom of God in Galilee. He calls his first 4 followers who were fishermen Simon, Andrew, James, and John.

The word **"midnight"** appears in the 13th chapter of Mark, in the 35th verse.

Watch ye therefore:
for ye know not when the master of the house cometh,
at even, or at midnight, or at the
cockcrowing, or in the morning:
Lest coming suddenly, he finds you sleeping.

Mark 13:35 – 36 KJV

The 13th chapter of Mark has 37 verses which can be outlined as follow. Jesus is speaking about the future and the signs of the end times.

1. The Destruction of the Temple, verses 1 – 2
2. Warning about Troubles, verses 3 – 13
3. The Abomination of Desolation, verses 14 – 23
4. When the Son of Man Appears, verses 24 – 27
5. A Lesson from a Fig Tree, verses 28 – 31
6. No One Know the Day or Hour, verses 32 - 37

In the passage of scriptures where the word **"midnight"** is embedded, Jesus is telling the people to Be ready! Be alert! Keep watch! It's a warning to prepare for the coming Christ. In this section, it's a short illustrative parable about being ready, alert, and watchful.

Beginning at verse 32, Jesus makes a point that no one, neither prophets nor angels, not even Jesus himself knows the day or hour of his return. Jesus gives a parable about the master leaves his house in the care of his servants. Each has their assigned task to do while the master is away. He expects them to carry out their assigned task faithfully.

The master commands the doorkeeper to keep watch, wait, and to open the door at the master's return. The master of the house can return at any time, so there is no time to be idle or sitting back doing nothing. According to verse 35, the master could return at any one of the 4 watches which are evening, **midnight**, at the crowing of the rooster or in the morning. If he comes unexpectedly, don't be found sleeping. This section ends with this verse.

And what I say to you, I say to all: Watch.
Mark 13:37 DRA

Note of Interests: While researching the scriptures, I discovered that Douay-Rheims 1899 American Edition (DRA), Darby Translation (DARBY), American Standard Version (ASV), and World English Bible (WEB) are Public Domain. However, the King James Version (KJV) is the most well-known of these. Praise God!

Throughout, the Gospel of Mark it narrated the miraculous nature of Jesus' ministry to the end. In chapter 14, 15, and 16, Mark speaks on Jesus betrayed by Judas, the distorted trial, Jesus beaten unmercifully, humiliated, crucified, buried, and His resurrection and ascension.

The Gospel of Mark ends on the ascension of the Lord Jesus to the right hand of God, and the Apostles are going forth to preach the word of the Lord with signs and wonders following, Mark 16:19 – 20.

CHAPTER 11

The Middle of the Night

**Then Jesus said to them,
"Suppose you have a friend, and you
go to him at midnight and say,
Friend, lend me three loaves of bread."**
Luke 11:5 NIV

The Gospel of Luke is one of the 4 Canonical Gospels in the New Testament, and the others are Matthew, Mark, and John. The Gospel of Matthew has the most chapters in comparison to the other 3 canonical gospels.

The Gospel of Matthew has 28 chapters while the Gospel of Mark has 16, Luke has 24, and John has 21. However, Luke's gospel is the longest of the gospels compared to words. It has approximately 19,482 words compared to Matthew with the most chapters with only 18,346 words.

The Gospel of Luke was written at the end of the 1st century by Luke, the physician. Christianity had become a worldwide gospel teaching, started in Jerusalem, Judea, and Samaria. Luke was not an eyewitness of the events in his Gospel, but much of what he wrote about in the Book of Acts. He collected the information from eyewitnesses, and most of it probably came from the Apostles and other disciples. Luke became a disciple of the Apostle Paul whom he followed, traveled, and supported until his martyrdom. Most of the Gospel of Mark is included in the Gospel of Luke, but not in the same order.

The Gospel of Luke and the Book of Acts were both written by Luke, and they are addressed to a Christian named Theophilus. Theophilus means "friend of God." Luke wrote to Theophilus to present to him an official narrative of the birth, life, ministry, death, resurrection, and ascension of Jesus Christ, as well as, the early history of the Christian movement.

Note of Interests: Luke was the only Gentile writer of the Bible. Luke, a disciple of the Apostle Paul, later became an Evangelist to the Gentiles. Luke was also an artist, creating more than 600 pictures which included the Blessed Virgin Mary. St. Luke's Feast Day is the 18th of October.

The Gospel of Luke records many more parables than the other gospels, a total of 24. Luke is the only gospel that describes the ascension of Jesus.

Luke was well-educated in Greek culture. He was born in Antioch, Syria which was around 300 miles north of Jerusalem. Antioch was a thriving center of trade around the Mediterranean Sea. It was ranked the 3rd importance after Rome and Alexandria. Antioch was known as the "Queen of the East."

After Stephen's martyrdom in Jerusalem, many of Jesus' followers fled the city and settled in Antioch. Antioch is the place where the word "Christian" was used and it's known as the "cradle of Christianity."

The 11th chapter of Luke has 54 verses, and it can be divided into 8 sections. They are listed below.

1. Jesus Teach His Disciples How to Pray to the Father, verses 1 – 4
2. Keep Asking, and You Will Receive, verses 5 – 13
3. A House Divided, verses 14 – 23
4. An Unclean Spirit Returns, verses 24 – 26
5. True Blessedness, verses 27 – 28
6. The Sign of Jonah, verses 29 – 32
7. The Lamp and Lampstand, verses 33 – 36
8. Woes Upon the Pharisees by Jesus, verses 37 – 54

The 2nd section titled, "Keep Asking and You Will Receive" is where the word **"midnight"** is embedded. This section of 9 verses is a parable Jesus spoke to his disciples after he had finished teaching them to pray.

Jesus said to his disciples, "Suppose one of you has a friend, and go to him at **midnight** to ask him to lend you 3 loaves of bread because a friend of yours has arrived for a visit, and you have nothing to give to him to eat." And suppose the person inside the house said, "do not disturb me for the door is shut. I am in bed with my children, and I cannot get up and give you bread."

The person inside the house will not get up and give you the bread, just because you are his friend, yet because you are persistence and not ashamed to keep on asking, he will rise and give you the bread.

Note of Interests: Hospitality was a unique custom in the Middle East. A man without bread for a visitor is disgraceful. The need for bread for a visitor would drive a man to his neighbor's house at **midnight** and cause him to be persistence in requesting bread.

Jesus then said, "I tell you, ask, and it will be given to you. Keep on seeking, and ye shall find. Keep on knocking, and the door will be opened to you. For everyone who asks, receives. Everyone who seeks, finds. And to everyone who knocks, the door will be opened," Luke 11:9 – 10.

Jesus then asked a question in this parable: "What fathers among you, if his son asks for a fish, will give him a snake, instead? Or if he asks for an egg, will you give him a scorpion? If you then, who are evil and sinful know how to give good gifts to your children, how much more will your heavenly Father give the Holy Spirit to those who ask him?" Luke 11:11 – 13.

CHAPTER 12
Paul and Silas

And at midnight Paul and Silas prayed,
and sang praises unto God:
and the prisoners heard them.
Acts 16:25 KJV

The Book of Acts is known as the Acts of the Apostles. It is the 5th book of the New Testament that records the works of the Apostles and the founding of the Christian church. The Book of Acts is the 2nd book written by Luke, addressed to Theophilus, and considered a continuation to Luke's Gospel. The Book of Acts by some scholars is called the 5th Gospel.

Many biblical scholars describe the Book of Acts and the Gospel of Luke as a two-part work called Luke-Acts. The first part which is the Gospel of Luke records how God fulfilled his plan for the world's salvation through the promised Messiah, Jesus Christ of Nazareth. The Book of Acts continues the events that surround the spread of Christianity in the 1st century.

The Book of Acts records how the Holy Spirit empowered believers, the spread of the Gospel of Jesus Christ, prayers prayed, miracles performed, and laid down the foundation for the future church. The history of the birth, the establishment and the spread of the church from Jerusalem to Rome are embedded in the Book of Acts.

The Book of Acts which is often referred to as simply, "Acts," contains 28 chapters. The influential individuals mentioned in the Book of Acts are Peter, Paul, John, James, Stephen, Barnabas, Timothy, Lydia, Silas, Apollos, Priscilla, and Aquila.

Acts 1 – 6: It records how the Holy Spirit empowered believers on the day of Pentecost. The sermon by Apostle Peter to the Jews who gather for the Feast of Weeks, resulting in 3,000 new believers in Jesus Christ. The early stages and development of the church in Jerusalem are recorded in this section.

Acts 6 – 9: The focus of evangelism to other areas are mentioned in this section. The ministry continued in Jerusalem. In Acts 8, Philip traveled down to Samaria and began proclaiming Christ to them. While Stephen preached to the religious leaders, he is stoned to death. As Stephen was being stoned, his executioners laid their robes at the feet of a young persecutor named Saul, who later became known as "Paul the Apostle." Saul spent his early days punishing and imprisoning Christians until he had a life's changing experience with Jesus Christ on the road to Damascus, Acts 9.

Acts 9 – 12: Evangelism of the gospel continue and begins in other territories. Peter received a revelation that the gospel was to be shared among the Gentiles, also. Cornelius, a Roman Commander, became a follower of Christ, and Saul, the persecutor, became a passionate follower.

Note of Interests: The term "Christians" is first used by the pagans living in Antioch, a city in the Roman Empire, Acts 11:26. The word was used to label the followers of Jesus Christ. The word "Christians" is mentioned only once in the KJV Bible, and the word "Christian" is mentioned twice, Acts 26:28 and 1 Peter 4:16. Antioch was one of the places the earliest Christians fled to, in order to escape persecution in Jerusalem.

Acts 12 – 15: Saul started using his Latin name, Paul. Paul and Barnabas begin their first and second missionary journeys to the Gentile world to preach the gospel of Jesus Christ. The missionary journey was successful, even though they faced many oppositions. In chapter 15, the Jerusalem Council takes place that authorized the spreading of the gospel message to the Gentile nations.

Acts 16 – 19: Paul receives a vision, after he was forbidden to enter Asia. He and Silas head farther West to Macedonia to preach the gospel in the Gentile European regions. Lydia, a woman who sold purple fabric, became the first convert along with her entire household. Paul preached to the Greek philosophers on Mars Hill and next sets out on his third missionary journey.

The word of the Lord was growing mightily and prevailing.

So mightily grew the word of God and prevailed.
Acts 19:20 KJV

In chapter 16 of Acts, verses 16 – 40 is the biblical event of Paul and Silas being put in jail, and between these verses is where the word **"midnight"** is embedded, verse 25.

In brief, Paul and Silas were going to the place of prayer when they were met by a slave girl with the spirit of divination. She made a substantial profit for her master by fortune-telling. She followed behind Paul and his traveling companions, crying out that these men were servants of the Most-High God for many days.

One day Paul became annoyed and said to the spirit in her, "I command you in the name of Jesus Christ to come out of her!" The spirit came out of her. The girl's masters saw that their hope of making money was gone because she couldn't foretell the future, anymore.

Paul and Silas were seized and dragged before the rulers. They were accused of disturbing the city by promoting customs that were unlawful for Romans. The city officials ordered them to be stripped and beaten with rods. Paul and Silas were then thrown in prison and placed in the inner cell. The jailer fastened their feet in leg irons.

At **midnight,** Paul and Silas were praying, praising, and singing hymns to God while the other prisoners were listening to them. All at once, there was an earthquake that shook the foundation of the prison. Suddenly, at once, all the prison doors flew open, and the chains of every prisoner fell off.

The jailer immediately woke up. He saw the prison doors open, and assumed the prisoners had all escaped. He was about to kill himself when Paul called out in a loud voice, "Do not harm yourself! We are all here!" The jailer kneels before Paul and Silas, and asked, "What must I do to be saved?" They replied, "Believe in the Lord Jesus, and you will be saved, you and your household."

Paul and Silas' wounds were washed, the jailer took them to his home, and prepared a meal for them. The jailer and his household were baptized, and they rejoiced because they had come to believe in God.

The next morning, the city official ordered the release of Paul and Silas, and they went to Lydia's house to see the followers and encourage them; afterward, they left the area.

Acts 19 – 28: These chapters describe Paul's travel to Jerusalem where he was arrested. His arduous journey to Rome for his trial. There in Rome, Paul is imprisoned and placed on house arrest. The Book of Acts abruptly ends without describing the event of Paul's trial before Caesar. These last two verses of the final chapter of Acts, read:

**For the next two years, Paul lived in
Rome at his own expense.
He welcomed all who visited him,
boldly proclaiming the Kingdom of God and
teaching about the Lord Jesus Christ.
And no one tried to stop him.**
Acts 28:30 – 31 NLT

CHAPTER 13

Paul Spoke

> **On the first day of the week,**
> **we gathered with the local believers**
> **to share in the Lord's Supper.**
> **Paul was preaching to them,**
> **and since he was leaving the next day,**
> **he kept talking until midnight.**
> Acts 20:7 NLT

Remember, the word **"midnight"** is mentioned the most in the Book of Acts; 3 times? Each biblical event surrounding the word **"midnight"** involves Apostle Paul. Beginning in Acts 20, Paul said, his good-byes to the believers in Troas and left for Macedonia.

Note of Interests: Troas is where Paul saw a vision of a "Man of Macedonia" who said, "Come over and help us," Acts 16:8 – 11. Paul obeyed the vision and much happened in Macedonia: Lydia became a disciple of Jesus, Acts 15:14 – 15; a slave girl was delivered, Acts 16:16 – 18; a jailer's household became believers, Acts 16:29 – 34; Paul preached at Areopagus, Acts 17:16 – 34, etc.

In the biblical event concerning Paul's last visit in Troas is where the word **"midnight"** is embedded. Paul had traveled to Troas to minister to the disciples and share the Lord's Supper with them before he departed. He was preaching in depths to them, and since he was leaving the next day. Paul just kept preaching until **midnight**.

The believers had gathered in the upper room with burning lamps. A young man named Eutychus was seated in the windowsill and fell asleep as Paul spoke. He fell from the 3rd loft window, and when the people there picked him up, he was dead.

Paul went down to Eutychus and took him in his arms. Paul said to the people, "Don't be alarmed! He is still alive." Paul raises Eutychus from the dead, and went back upstairs, broke bread, ate, and continue preaching until daybreak. The name "Eutychus" means "fortunate."

Acts, chapter 20 ends with Paul sending a message for the church leaders at Ephesus to meet with him. He speaks with them about his work for the Lord. When he finished speaking, he knelt with all of them and prayed.

Note of Interests: On Paul's 2nd missionary journey, the history of the church at Ephesus begins, Acts 18:18 – 28. Priscilla and Aquila accompanied Paul to Ephesus, and he proclaimed Christ in their synagogue. He was asked to stay to teach further, but he declined and promised to return later. Paul returned to Ephesus and stayed approximately 3 years. He taught first, in the synagogue for 3 months, when opposition aroused, he taught at the School of Tyrannus, Acts 19:8 – 10. Later, Timothy led the church in Ephesus, 1 Timothy 1:3. Paul sent Timothy, the young pastor, 2 letters to instruct him in the ways of church leadership and to encourage him.

Don't Forget . . . Paul the Apostle made 4 missionary journeys which are mentioned in the Book of Acts. Paul's 1st missionary journey was with Barnabas, Acts 13:4 – 15:35. Scholars believe it was in the year 47 AD when Paul started in Syria and traveled to Cyprus and Asia Minor (Ephesus, Smyrna, Pergamos, Thyatira, Sardis, Philadelphia, Laodicea).

Paul 2nd missionary journey began in the spring of 49 AD, and it was with Silas, Acts 15:36 – 18:22. He set out from Antioch, Syria to visit the churches he had established in Asia Minor (Ephesus, Smyrna, Pergamos, Thyatira, Sardis, Philadelphia, Laodicea) on his 1st journey.

On Paul's 3rd missionary journey, he went to Galatia, Phrygia, Macedonia, Greece and crossed into Caesarea and Jerusalem, Acts 18:23 – 21:17. On this journey, he went to strengthen the followers and believers in cities where he had already been.

According to Acts 27:1 – 28:16, Paul, along with other prisoners, aboard a ship for Rome is considered his 4th missionary journey. Although Paul was a prisoner in Rome, he lived by himself, guarded by a Roman soldier. He received visitors and continues to preach the gospel, even to the Jewish religious leaders in Rome, Acts 28:17 – 29.

CHAPTER 14

Paul Don't be Afraid!

**But when the fourteenth night was come,
as we were driven up and down in Adria,
about midnight the shipmen deemed that
they drew near to some country.**
Acts 27:27 KJV

Remember, the Book of Acts is the 5th book in the New Testament written by Luke. It has 28 chapters that give an account of the birth and growth of the church. The 27th chapter of Acts is the 3rd place where the word **"midnight"** is found in the Book of Acts. This chapter has 44 verses and can be outlined as follow.

1. Paul Sails to Rome, verses 1 – 12
2. The Storm at Sea, verses 13 – 38
3. The Shipwreck, verses 39 – 44

This chapter is about Paul and prisoners on a ship that had set sail to Rome. In the course of the journey, a storm arose at sea, they became shipwreck and had to swim to land. The 27th verse of Acts 27 regarding "The Storm at Sea" reads:

**About midnight on the fourteenth night of the storm,
as we were being driven across the Sea of Adria,
the sailors sensed land was near.**
Acts 27:27 NLT

In brief, beginning at Acts 27, Paul a prisoner, along with several other prisoners were handed over to a centurion named Julius. They were to sail to Italy, and port along the coast of Asia on the way. When the ship docked in Sidon, Julius allowed Paul's friends to visit with him, and provide for his needs.

When they left Sidon, they encountered strong winds that made it difficult to keep the ship on course. The shipmen decided to sail close to the northern coast of the island of Cyprus for safety. When they came to Myra in Lycia, the commanding officer found an Alexandrian ship sailing for Italy and the prisoners were placed on board, Acts 27:6.

They sailed slowly for several days and finally arrived off the town of Cnidus. The wind prevented them from going any farther, so they sailed near Crete. They finally came to a place called Fair Havens, near the town of Lasea.

Since considerable time had been lost because of the weather and the journey was becoming dangerous for it was so late in the fall. Paul warns those on the ship that he believes that trouble was ahead, not only to the ship and cargo but to their own lives as well. However, the centurion in charge of the prisoners listened to the ship's captain, Acts 27:11.

The harbor of Fair Havens was an excellent location to spend the winter. Most of the men decided to set sail from there hoping to reach Phoenix, a harbor on the island of Crete to spend the winter there. When a gentle wind from the south began to blow, the men thought their plan would work. They raised the anchor and started sailing along the shore of Crete. Soon there arose a violent stormy wind called the Euroclydon that drove the ship off course, Acts 27:14.

The next day the violent storm continued, and the storm severely battered them. The men began to lighten the ship by throwing some of the cargo overboard. On the 3rd day of the storm, the crew cast extra ship overboard. The storm raged for many days, neither sun nor stars could be seen. The violent wind kept blowing, and the crew finally gave up all hope of being saved, Acts 27:20.

Paul stood amid the crew after they had been without food for a long time. He told them; they should have followed his advice not to sail from Crete they would have escaped this disaster. Paul told them to take courage, and none of their lives will be lost, only the ship. Just last night an angel of the God he serves, stood by him. The angel told Paul, don't be afraid because he must stand trial before Caesar. God in his goodness has granted safety to everyone sailing with him. However, we will be ship wrecked and stranded on an island, Acts 27:26.

The word **"midnight"** appears in the next verse, and it reads.

**On the fourteenth night
we were still being driven across the Adriatic Sea,
when about midnight the sailors sensed
they were approaching land.**
Acts 27:27 NIV

The shipmen cast an anchor into the water, twice. The second time, the anchor sank 90 ft. deep. They feared they would run aground upon rocks, so they dropped 4 anchors from the stern and wished for daybreak, Acts 27:29.

Some shipmen wanted to escape from the ship. They lowered the lifeboat in the sea pretending that they would lay out anchors from the foreship. Paul said to Julius, soldiers, and other shipmen, "unless these men stayed on board of the ship, you have no hope of being saved." The soldiers cut the ropes to the lifeboat, and it drifted away, Acts 27:32.

Just before daylight, Paul urged the men to eat something. He said, "This is the 14th day that you have fasted; not a single hair from your head will be lost." After Paul spoke these words, he took some bread, gave thanks to God in the presence of them all, broke it in pieces, and began to eat. They were all encouraged, and 276 who were on board ate, too, Acts 27:38.

When daylight came, they saw a bay with a beach that they didn't recognize. They decided to run the ship ashore there. The shipmen cut away the anchors, loosened the ropes that held the rudders, raised the foresail, and headed toward shore, but the ship struck a sandbar and ran aground to soon. The front of the ship wouldn't move; it was firmly stuck in the sand. The rear of the ship was smashed by the violent waves, breaking it into pieces, Acts 27:41.

Now, the soldiers planned to kill the prisoners, in order to keep them from swimming ashore and escaping. The centurion wanted to spare Paul's life. He immediately ordered those who could swim to jump overboard first and swim to shore. Those who couldn't swim were to hold on to planks, and ship pieces that were floating on the sea. And it came to pass that they were all saved, Acts 27:44.

And the rest,
some on boards, and some on broken pieces of the ship.
And so it came to pass,
that they escaped all safe to the land.
Acts 27:44 KJV

PS: The last chapter of Acts, Chapter 28, is just as captivating.

A READER'S QUESTION

This new section just dropped in my spirit at 0613 on January 14, 2017, titled <u>A Reader's Question</u>.

An individual asked me the following question:
"Which of your books do you like the most?"

<u>The Answer</u>:
I don't have a favorite book.
However, "Perfect Peace V" is the most personal.
It speaks about my parents, has a picture of my dad in his army uniform, and a group picture of my youngest sister and me with our mom and dad.
The front and back cover of this book is actually, their resting place.

In all thy ways acknowledge him, and
He shall direct thy paths.
Proverbs 3:6

AUTHOR'S CLOSING REMARKS

I hope you enjoyed the book.

Espero que hayan disfrutado el libro.

⁕⁕◆⦿◆⁕⁕

Pray for the Ministry . . . May the "LORD of Peace," give you His Peace.

Dr. Vanessa

REFERENCES

Chapter 1
1. BibleGateway: https://www.biblegateway.com

Chapter 2
1. BibleGateway: https://www.biblegateway.com
2. Jacksonville Theology Seminary: Moses

Chapter 3
1. Jacksonville Theology: Passover

Chapter 4
1. BibleGateway: https://www.biblegateway.com
2. Wikipedia, The Free Encyclopedia: https://en.wikipedia.
    org/wiki/History of Gaza

Chapter 5
1. Wikipedia, The Free Encyclopedia: https://en.wikipedia.
    org/wiki/Boaz
2. BibleGateway: https://www.biblegateway.com

Chapter 6
1. BibleGateway: https://www.biblegateway.com
2. Jacksonville Theology Seminary: Solomon
3. Wikipedia, The Free Encyclopedia: https://en.wikipedia.
    org/wiki/Gibeon

Chapter 7
1. Wikipedia, The Free Encyclopedia: https://en.wikipedia.org/wiki/Elihu
2. BibleGateway: https://www.biblegateway.com

Chapter 8
1. Wikipedia, The Free Encyclopedia: https://en.wikipedia.org/wiki/Psalms
2. Jacksonville Theology Seminary: Psalms

Chapter 9
1. Wikipedia, The Free Encyclopedia: https://en.wikipedia.org/wiki/Bridegroom
2. BibleGateway: https://www.biblegateway.com

Chapter 10
1. Wikipedia, The Free Encyclopedia: https://en.wikipedia.org/wiki/Gospel_of_Mark
2. BibleGateway: https://www.biblegateway.com
3. Jacksonville Theology Seminary: Gospel of Mark

Chapter 11
1. BibleGateway: https://www.biblegateway.com
2. Jacksonville Theology Seminary: Gospel of Luke
3. Wikipedia, The Free Encyclopedia: https://en.wikipedia.org/wiki/Gospel_of_Luke

Chapter 12
1. Wikipedia, The Free Encyclopedia: https://en.wikipedia.org/wiki/Acts_of_the_Apostles
2. Jacksonville Theology Seminary: Acts of the Apostles
3. BibleGateway: https://www.biblegateway.com

Chapter 13
1. Wikipedia, The Free Encylopedia: https://en.wikipedia.org/wiki/Paul the Apostle
2. BibleGateway: https://www.biblegateway.com
3. Jacksonville Theology Seminary: Paul's Missionary Journeys

Chapter 14
1. BibleGateway: https://www.biblegateway.com
2. Jacksonville Theology Seminary: Apostle Paul

ANSWERS & INFORMATION SECTION

Chapter 4
Delilah was paid 1,1000 pieces of silver by each of the lords of the Philistines which was 5; Judges 16:5, Judges 3:3. Scholars believe that calculated to be $89,641, in today times.

Chapter 5
The Book of Esther
The Book of Judith has 16 chapters and its part of the Old Testament of the Catholic Bible. Catholic Bibles have 7 more books in the Old Testament than Protestant Bibles. These books are known as the "Apocrypha" or "Deuterocanonical." The word "Apocrypha" means "hidden." The Book of Judith records how God empowered a wise, beautiful widow to deliver the Jewish people from King Nebuchadnezzar powerful general named Holofernes.

Chapter 9
1. *Myrrh
2. Frankincense
3. Cedarwood
4. *Cinnamon
5. *Cassia
6. *Calamus
7. Galbanum

8. Onycha
9. Spikenard
10. Hyssop
11. Sandalwood
12. Myrtle
13. Cypress
14. Rose of Sharon
15. *Olive Oil
16. Aloe

*The oils the Lord gave to Moses as a recipe for a "holy anointing oil."

The wise men brought the child Christ frankincense and myrrh.

Mary, the sister of Lazarus and Martha anointed Jesus' feet with expensive oil of spikenard 6 days before he was crucified.

OTHER BOOKS BY THE AUTHOR

ABOUT THE AUTHOR

Vanessa Rayner is the author of nineteen books in which eighteen are in a series called "Perfect Peace." She writes biblical information uniquely and profoundly, striving to help keep your mind on Father God throughout the entire day. She attended Jacksonville Theological Seminary where she received a doctorate in Ministry. She has been taught by the Holy Spirit, trained by experiences, tried by adversity and tested by fire.

Printed in the United States
By Bookmasters